DATE DUE

ASANTE

THE KINGDOMS OF AFRICA

ASANTE

THE GOLD COAST

PHILIP KOSLOW

CHELSEA HOUSE PUBLISHERS • New York • Philadelphia

Frontispiece: A view of the coastline along the Gulf of Guinea in the present-day nation of Ghana. During the great days of the Asante empire, European ships sailed to this coast in search of gold.

On the Cover: An artist's interpretation of a gold Akan mask; in the background, a scene from the annual Odwira Festival in Kumase, the capital of the Asante empire.

CHELSEA HOUSE PUBLISHERS
Editorial Director Richard Rennert
Executive Managing Editor Karyn Gullen Browne
Copy Chief Robin James
Picture Editor Adrian J. Allen
Creative Director Robert Mitchell
Production Manager Sallye Scott
Art Director Joan Ferrigno

THE KINGDOMS OF AFRICA
Senior Editor Martin Schwabacher

Staff for ASANTE
Assistant Editor Catherine Iannone
Editorial Assistant Erin McKenna
Senior Designer Cambraia Magalhães
Picture Researcher Lisa Kirchner
Cover Illustrator Bradford Brown

First Printing
1 3 5 7 9 8 6 4 2

Library of Congress Cataloging-in-Publication Data
Koslow, Philip.
   Asante: The Gold Coast / Philip Koslow.
   p. cm. — (The Kingdoms of Africa)
Includes bibliographical references and index.
Summary : Provides information on the history and people of the Kingdom of Asante.
   ISBN 0-7910-3139-X
      0-7910-3140-3.(pbk)
1. Ashanti (Kingdom)—Juvenile literature. 2. Akan (African people)—Juvenile literature.
[1. Ashanti (Kingdom)—History. 2. Akan (African people)] I. Title. II. Series.
DT507.K67 1996   966.7018—dc20
95-9440   CIP
                                                            AC

CONTENTS

Titles in
THE KINGDOMS OF AFRICA

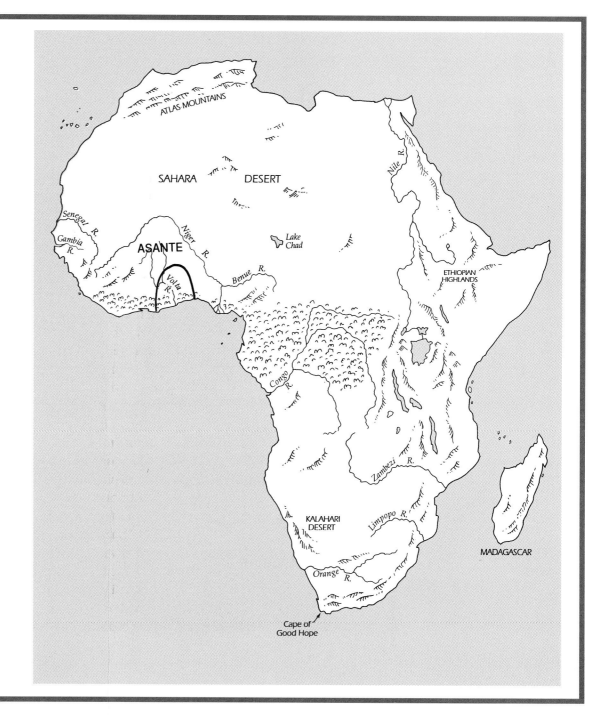

"CIVILIZATION AND MAGNIFICENCE"

On a sunny morning in July 1796, Mungo Park, a Scottish doctor turned explorer, achieved a major goal of his long and difficult trek through West Africa when he reached the banks of the mighty Niger River. Along the river was a cluster of four large towns, which together made up the city of Segu, the principal settlement of the Bambara people. The sight of Segu dazzled Park as much as the spectacle of the broad, shining waterway. "The view of this extensive city," he wrote, "the numerous canoes upon the river; the crowded population; and the cultivated state of the surrounding country, formed altogether a prospect of civilization and magnificence, which I little expected to find in the bosom of Africa."

Park's account of his journey, *Travels in the Interior Districts of Africa*, became a best-seller in England. But his positive reflections on Africa were soon brushed aside by the English and other Europeans, who were engaged in a profitable trade in slaves along the West African coast and were eventually to carve up the entire continent into colonies. Later explorers such as Richard Burton, who spoke of the "childishness" and "backwardness" of Africans, achieved more lasting fame than did Park, who drowned during a second expedition to Africa in 1806. Thus it is not surprising that 100 years after Park's arrival at Segu, a professor at England's Oxford University could write with bland self-assurance that African history before the arrival of Europeans had been nothing more than "blank, uninteresting, brutal barbarism." The professor's opinion was published

A relief map of Africa indicating the territory once controlled by the Asante empire.

7

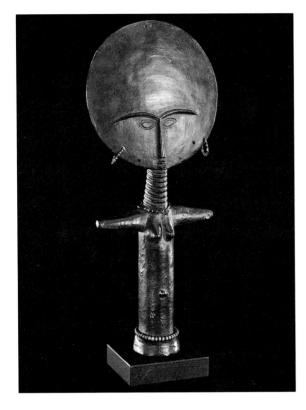

A fertility doll (akua'mma) carved by an Asante artist. Akua'mma are said to help women conceive and to ensure the birth of healthy children.

when the British Empire was at its height, and it represented a point of view that was necessary to justify the exploitation of Africans. If, as the professor claimed, Africans had lived in a state of chaos throughout their history, then their European conquerors could believe that they were doing a noble deed by imposing their will and their way of life upon Africa.

The colonialist view of African history held sway into the 20th century. But as the century progressed, more enlightened scholars began to take a fresh look at Africa's past. As archaeologists (scientists who study the physical remains of past societies) explored the sites of former African cities, they found that Africans had enjoyed a high level of civilization hundreds of years before the arrival of Europeans. In many respects, the kingdoms and cities of Africa had been equal to or more advanced than European societies during the same period.

As early as the 5th century B.C. when ancient Greece was enjoying its Golden Age, West African peoples had developed a highly sophisticated way of life and were producing magnificent works of art. By A.D. 750, ancient Ghana, known as the Land of Gold, emerged as West Africa's first centralized kingdom. When Ghana began to decline in the 12th century, power shifted to the empire of Mali, where the great ruler Mansa Musa became legendary for his wealth, generosity, and refinement. After the 15th century, Mali's grandeur passed to Songhay, which controlled the great trading cities of Gao, Jenne, and Timbuktu; to the dual kingdom of Kanem-Borno, whose ruling dynasty controlled the shores of Lake Chad for 1,000 years; and to the remarkable fortress kingdoms of Hausaland, whose armored horsemen displayed their valor on the sunbaked plains. These great nations were located in the heartland of West Africa, the wide savanna that borders the vast Sahara Desert. To a large extent, the savanna kingdoms owed their wealth and grandeur to trade with North Africa and the Middle East. Because of this ever-widening economic and cultural contact, the fame of the Bilad al-Sudan ("land of the black peoples" in Arabic) spread throughout the world.

However, the rich saga of the savanna states does not represent the entire history of West African achievement. Indeed, much of the savanna's wealth derived from the gold and ivory supplied by the peoples of the lush forest belt that extends along the southern coast of West Africa. The forest-land communities, such as those of Yorubaland and Benin, had established themselves at least as early as those of the savanna, but because of their distant location and rugged terrain they were largely unknown to outsiders until the arrival of European mariners in the 15th century. The history of the forest states forms a unique chapter in the development of African civilization, and some of the most remarkable contributions to that saga were made by the kingdom of Asante, which flourished in the gold-rich valley of the Volta River.

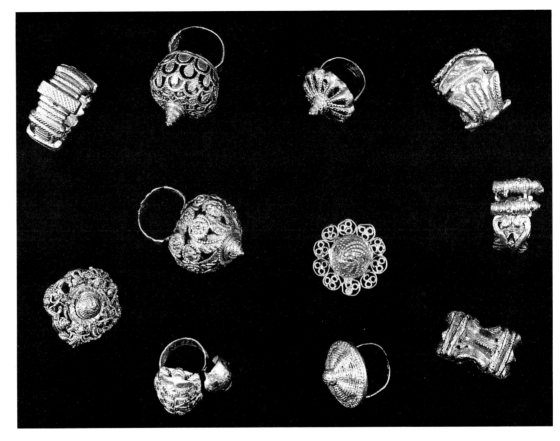

A selection of gold finger and toe rings from 19th-century Asante. The exquisite artworks produced by Africans attest to the refinement of their civilizations.

Chapter 1 | THE PATH AND THE STREAM

In the Akan forest, dense undergrowth and towering trees create a perpetual gloom, blocking the sun even at midday. The Akan have long believed that the forest shelters supernatural creatures who can, according to their mood, annihilate humans or endow them with magical powers.

Like all of Africa's more than 800 ethnic groups, the Asante of present-day Ghana have a keen sense of their past. Their collective history, only recently written down, has been preserved for centuries in spoken narratives passed from generation to generation. Among the most revealing traditions are the verses that reflect on the mysteries of creation:

> The stream crosses the path,
> The path crosses the stream;
> Which of them is the elder?
> Did we not cut a path to go
>   and meet this stream?
> The stream had its origin
>   long long ago.
> The stream had its origin in
>   the Creator.

The Asante know the exact spot where the stream of creation crossed the path of human history: the sacred grove of Asantemanso, sheltered in the dense forest where few outsiders dare to venture. Standing in this grove during the 1920s, the queen mother of the Asante told a privileged visitor about the origins of the first Asante clan, the Oyoko, whose descendants later ruled the nation:

> Very long ago upon a certain Monday night a worm bored its way up through the ground and was followed by seven men, several women, a leopard, and a dog. . . . All these people, with one exception (Adu Ogyinae), were distracted by the new and strange sights that they saw around them, and their eyes roved wildly about in fear. Adu Ogyinae lay his hands upon them one by one and soothed them. By Wednesday they had begun to build

huts, but while so engaged a tree fell upon Adu Ogyinae and killed him. . . . The dog went away and brought back fire in his mouth, food was laid upon the fire, and the dog was fed with this (as an experiment), and as it grew fat, men came to eat cooked food.

The exact date of the first Asante settlement has not been determined, but the

An iron knife used by the Akan during their early history, when they lived as wandering hunter-gatherers.

Asante have occupied their forest homeland for several thousand years. In earliest times, they lived as hunter-gatherers and called themselves the Akan, which was the name of their language. (Though African peoples have widely differing physical characteristics, they are identified principally by the language they speak.) The Akan harvested wild plant foods and lived on the meat of such creatures as monkeys, antelope, and giant snails, all of which were plentiful in the forest. When they found a clearing amid the thick undergrowth and giant trees, some of which grew to a height of 200 feet, they could use their stone tools to plant crops and build small villages. But for many centuries, even after they learned to make more efficient tools from iron, the enveloping forest thwarted their progress. A dramatic impression of the daunting landscape occupied by the Akan was rendered by a 19th-century European visitor: "Few people . . . can understand the loathing with which one regards the endless monotony of the forest, through the dank vegetation of which one moves day after day as if between two lofty walls of foliage, without seeing a single glade or break in the sameness."

12

Foreigners were not alone in feeling intimidated by the gloom of the forest. The Akan themselves were in awe of their surroundings, as Malcolm McLeod has indicated in his 1981 book *The Asante:*

> The bush was an area of disorder, potential power and danger. Besides being the home of wild beasts, it was the home of such superhuman beings as *sasabonsam* and *mmoatia. Sasabonsam* was believed to be a great hairy red beast which lived in the tallest trees. A combination of creatures from several realms with legs like snakes, wings like those of a bat, an ape-like body and a carnivore's head and teeth, it was believed to catch hunters with its long dangling legs and then devour them. . . . *Mmoatia* were envisaged as small and totally unpredictable goblin-like beings, red, white, or black, with backward-pointing feet, who either attacked or succoured hunters or others who became lost in the bush.

In addition to spirits and demons, the forest harbored more visible threats, such as the tsctsc fly, which transmitted the disease commonly known as sleeping sickness to both humans and animals, cutting down many people in their prime and making it impossible to breed cattle and horses.

Considering all these factors, the Akan homeland might seem one of the more unlikely places on earth for a great kingdom to flourish. But if the forest inflicted hardships on the Akan, it also offered some rare opportunities. The first arose from the abundance of kola trees, whose large nuts contain a stimulant similar to caffeine. The energy-boosting and thirst-quenching properties of the kola made it highly desirable in the hot West African climate. Inhabitants of the savanna, where water supplies are frequently scarce, were especially eager to obtain kola nuts. For this reason the Wangara, Muslim traders from the empire of Mali, began to journey south toward the forest belt. At least as early as the 14th century, they established a community at Begho in the northern sector of Akan country, and from there they transported kolas and other goods to the great trading cities along the Niger River.

Kolas were not the only prize sought by the enterprising Wangara. Mali, one of the wealthiest empires in world history, had built its glory by

13

14

The ruins of Elmina castle, built by Portuguese traders in 1482. Later taken over by the Dutch, Elmina remained an important source of trade for Asante until the end of the 19th century.

controlling the output of the world's richest goldfields, situated in the forest belt at Bambuk and Bure, west of Akan country. The trade in Mali's gold had enriched the sultans of Egypt and Arabia and had enabled the kings of Europe to raise their nations from the gloom of the Dark Ages. By the 14th century, however, the mines of Bambuk were approaching exhaustion, and the world's gold traders searched for new sources of wealth. They soon discovered that the Akan forestlands contained the richest lodes of all.

Guided by the expertise of migrants from Bambuk and Bure, the Akan began to exploit their goldfields during the 15th century. They traded the precious metal not only to the Wangara but also to the European explorers, mostly Portuguese, who reached the coast of Akan country in the 1470s and established a fort they called Elmina (the Mine). From their trading partners, the Akan received various goods, including iron, cutlery, salt, weapons, glassware, and cloth. Most important of all, they began to purchase slaves. The slaves were supplied both by the Portuguese, who acquired them from Benin farther down the coast, and by the Wangara, who offered captives taken in the wars and slave raids of the various savanna states. This trade in slaves provided the Akan with the labor they needed to build their communities.

In order to clear even a small plot of farmland in the virgin forest of Akan country, it was necessary to remove tons of vegetation, a backbreaking task for small groups of people equipped only with axes. Mining gold was equally arduous; there were no draft animals to haul ore, water, and debris out of the pits, and because the forest soil remained damp through much of the year, cave-ins were a constant menace.

With the importation of additional labor, these tasks became feasible. Large-scale farms could support an ever-increasing population, both free and slave, and the added manpower made it possible to extract ever-increasing quantities of gold from the earth. With the added gold, the Akan could purchase even more labor, and so on. This dynamic cycle of growth finally resulted in the birth of a great kingdom.

15

Chapter 2 | THE GOLDEN STOOL

During their early history, the Akan were grouped into clans (also known as descent lines), which consisted of individuals who traced their lineage to a common ancestor. Originally, each clan had its own plot of land and managed its own affairs. But as the Akan began to clear the forest and to farm on a large scale, groups from different clans might combine to create a larger village, raising livestock to supplement the crops they grew.

In a typical Akan village, people built the frames of their houses with cane stalks and lashed the stalks together with vines or strips of bark. Walls and roofs were constructed of tightly woven thatch that kept out the downpours of the rainy season, when the villagers had to wear raised wooden sandals to move about. In more prosperous villages, the walls of the houses were made of plaster and could be decorated with a smooth layer of clay that created a bright red sheen. The houses ran along both sides of the village's wide main street, nestling under the outspread branches of great shade trees that served as gathering places for the entire community. As Malcolm McLeod explains, the shade trees had special significance for the Akan:

> These trees were planted not merely to provide shade in a land where the fierce sun is almost vertically overhead for the middle part of the day; they were also connected with the concept of chiefship and with the spiritual "coolness" (dwo) or peace of the whole town. . . . On his accession a chief was expected to plant a new shade tree, the trees of

The outskirts of an Akan village, with a colossal tree dwarfing both the inhabitants and their houses. Akan villages were connected by a network of narrow paths winding through the forest.

his predecessors were decorated with white cloth, and before them he swore an oath to rule well and guard his people.

By the late 17th century, the Akan had made their unruly landscape so habitable that William Bosman, a Dutch merchant visiting the coastal region, wrote the following description:

[The country] abounds in hills, all enriched with extraordinary high and beautiful trees; its valleys betwixt the hills are wide and extensive, proper for the planting of all sorts of fruits. . . . The earth produceth, in great abundance, very good rice, the richest sort of millet the grain of which is red, jambs [yams], potatoes, and other fruits, all good in their kind; nor is the soil in the least deficient in fruit-trees.

One of these hilly regions, Adanse, contained the largest of the Akan goldfields. As the people of Adanse grew ever richer, they began to expand northward. Gradually, they occupied regions such as Kumase, Bekwae, Kokofu, Mampon, Dwaben, and Masuta, displacing and absorbing the former inhabitants. The men who became the chiefs of these settlements belonged to different branches of the great Oyoko clan, and the various Oyoko communities recognized their common kinship and spiritual heritage. At some point, they began to call themselves the Asante, after the sacred grove of Asantemanso, from which the Oyoko clan traces its origins. The chief of Kumase held the highest rank among the Asante; but during these early years many of the Asante remained loyal to their own chiefs and their own clans, and they were often unwilling to follow the lead of Kumase.

Because of their disunity, the Asante were not the most prominent of the Akan-speaking peoples. That distinction belonged to the Denkyira, who lived southwest of Adanse. Throughout

Akan villagers gather under a shade tree. Planted by village chiefs at the beginning of their tenure, such trees had great spiritual value—the Akan believed that the trees embodied the power of the chiefs and would protect the village from harm.

18

the 17th century, the Denkyira held sway over all their neighbors. They defeated the Asante in battle around 1650 and forced their vanquished foes to pay a yearly tribute. Though the Asante continued to prosper, they were unable to mount an effective challenge to the power of Denkyira—until the advent of Osei Tutu.

According to tradition, Osei Tutu actually lived for a number of years in Denkyira; his uncle Oti Akenten, the chief of Kumase, had sent him there, along with seven servants, as a hostage to ensure the continued payment of tribute. Osei Tutu married a Denkyira woman and even took part in Denkyira's military campaign against the state of Sehwi, during which he captured a substantial amount of gold from the enemy. Boamponsem, Denkyira's king, demanded that Osei Tutu surrender the gold to him. When Osei Tutu refused, Boamponsem seduced Osei Tutu's wife. Enraged by this insult, Osei Tutu swore vengeance against Boamponsem, fled Denkyira with his seven servants, and took refuge in the state of Akwamu, far to the east of Denkyira.

Meanwhile, Oti Akenten died, and Osei Tutu's brother Obiri Yeboa became chief of Kumase. When Obiri Yeboa was killed in battle against the nearby state of Domaa, the Asante chiefs sent a messenger to Akwamu and asked Osei Tutu to return and become their leader. When Osei Tutu received this summons, he quickly returned to Kumase with his seven servants and a priest named Anokye. He was prepared to accept the position of chief of Kumase, but he would not simply follow in the footsteps of his uncle and brother. Osei Tutu believed that rivalry between the various clans was preventing the Asante from becoming a great nation. His plan was to create a new unity by combining the religious beliefs of the Asante with their respect for the *akonnua*, or royal stool.

At a solemn ceremony in Kumase, attended by a huge crowd, Osei Tutu accepted the akonnua from the chiefs of the leading communities and agreed to be the ruler of the Asante. After Osei Tutu had observed the traditional rites, the priest Anokye came forward and announced that Onyame, the god of creation, wished the Asante to become a mighty nation. As a sign of his intentions, Anokye said, Onyame was sending a Golden Stool from

This wooden Asante stool, overlaid with strips of silver, was once the property of a senior government official. In Asante and other West African societies, stools represented the spiritual authority of their owners and were preserved for generations in family shrines.

heaven to serve as the Asante's national symbol. At this point, Anokye produced a wooden stool sheathed in a thin layer of gold. (According to tradition, the stool descended from heaven in a dense black cloud, while thunder rumbled and the air became thick with white dust.) Anokye then placed the stool upon the knees of Osei Tutu. The Golden Stool, Anokye proclaimed, contained the soul of the Asante people. If the stool were cherished and protected, the Asante would flourish; but if the stool were to be dishonored or surrendered to an enemy, the Asante would wither away like a person whose soul has been corrupted.

From this time on, the Golden Stool, known in Akan as the Sika Dwa, became a sacred object for the Asante. It was never allowed to touch the ground, and even the king was not allowed to sit on it. When he appeared at ceremonies he would sit on his wooden akonnua, place the Golden Stool next to him, and merely lean his arm on it. In the annual procession to the royal tombs, the Golden Stool was carried ahead of the king, shaded by a large umbrella and accompanied by even more attendants than the king himself.

An astute political leader, Osei Tutu reinforced the symbolic value of the Golden Stool by enacting concrete measures to promote unity. He was the first ruler to actually use the title *asantehene*, "chief of the Asante," reinforcing his leadership of the entire nation rather than just his own clan. In addition, Osei Tutu introduced a law forbidding his subjects to speak publicly about the history of their clans; it was only permissible to speak of the Asante people as a whole.

The new asantehene, who had learned much about the arts of war in Denkyira and Akwamu, spent three years building up Asante's army. When he had done so, he launched a successful campaign against Domaa, avenging his brother's death. During the 1680s, Asante's army (its major divisions commanded by Osei Tutu's seven servants) went on to defeat a number of neighboring peoples. Despite his desire for revenge against Boamponsem, however, Osei Tutu did not wage war on the still-powerful Denkyira, choosing the path of diplomacy instead. Boamponsem was also eager to avoid a ruinous conflict, and he responded to Osei Tutu's approaches by freeing the Asante from nearly all their tribute obligations. The two nations remained at peace until Boamponsem's death in 1694. At that point the new king of Denkyira sent an ambassador to Kumase, demanding a new tribute—the favorite son and wife of every Asante chief as well as a yearly payment of one brass pan filled with gold dust. The Asante were so offended by this extravagant demand that one of the chiefs flew into a rage and killed the emissary, violating the widely held custom that protected ambassadors from physical harm.

War between the two states was now inevitable. At the Battle of Feiyase, fought in 1701 just outside Kumase, Osei Tutu's forces resoundingly defeated

A war shirt belonging to a high-ranking Asante officer. The pouches sewn to the shirt contain safi, *Islamic writings designed to protect the wearer in battle.* Safi *were sold by Muslim traders and holy men who journeyed to Asante from the savanna states of the north.*

the Denkyira and gained the liberation of Asante. With "the towering pride of Dinkira in ashes" (as William Bosman put it), Asante emerged as the dominant power in the region that Europeans were already calling the Gold Coast. The stage was now set for the unified Asante to build one of the world's richest empires.

Chapter 3 | UNDER THE KUMA TREE

In the history of many nations, the death of a great leader has sometimes ushered in a period of instability or a gradual decline. This was not the case in Asante. Following the death of Osei Tutu in 1717, the kingdom continued to grow under the reign of outstanding rulers such as Opoku Ware and Osei Kwadwo.

Opoku Ware acceded to the Golden Stool in 1720 and quickly set about solidifying the gains made under Osei Tutu. Perhaps the most important measures taken by Opoku Ware were the creation of a national treasury and the initiation of death duties (awun-yyade), whereby the wealth of deceased citizens went into Asante's treasury. The Asante believed that the best citizens were those who worked

hard during their lifetime, leaving behind wealth that would enrich the nation.

The growing wealth of Asante was symbolized by the Golden Elephant Tail (Sika Mena), a gold-plated fly whisk that was carried by royal attendants along with the Golden Stool. In addition, one of the asantehene's officers always carried several bunches of keys, representing the vast number of locked strongboxes that were needed to hold the royal treasure. It was said that one of the asantehenes liked to hear these keys being rattled as he took his morning bath.

In addition to amassing revenue, Opoku Ware undertook a number of successful military campaigns. Under his direction, Asante influence spread

A street scene in Kumase, showing elaborately decorated dampans (government offices), a weaver working at a loom, and a merchant displaying his wares. The porches and steps of the buildings were covered with a layer of clay and polished until they took on a bright red sheen.

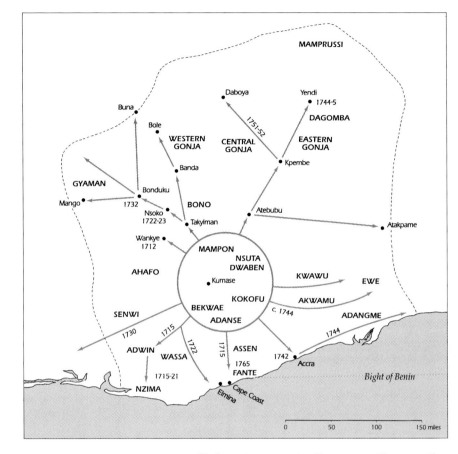

A map of the Asante empire. The various states under the control of Kumase are indicated in capital letters; arrows show the process of Asante expansion during the 18th century.

coast. There, the Dutch had taken over Elmina from the Portuguese, and the British had established a trading fort called Cape Coast Castle. By dealing with European merchants, the Asante were able to obtain manufactured goods such as iron and glassware directly from Europe without paying the higher prices demanded by Wangara middlemen. As their trade with Europe developed, however, the Asante were principally interested in obtaining firearms.

The Asante possessed a large army, and every able-bodied man accepted his responsibility to serve if called upon (During wartime, the women of a village would often parade up and down the main street for hours in a ceremony known as *mmumue*, chanting and lamenting as they imitated the military maneuvers of the absent men.) Naturally, the addition of firearms in place of spears during the 1680s made the Asante armies even more fearsome. Though the cumbersome guns of that era were difficult to load and often dangerous to fire, the Asante used them to great advantage. Typically, musketeers were deployed in the front ranks of the army, with archers and swordsmen backing them up. After

in all directions—to Gonja in the north, to Accra in the south, to Atakpame in the east, to Gyaman in the west—until the Asante controlled a territory of roughly 90,000 square miles.

During Opoku Ware's reign, the main focus of Asante's trade began to shift from the savanna states to the

(Continued on page 29)

24

THE GOLD OF ASANTE

Between 1500 and 1900, the mines of Asante yielded massive amounts of gold—as much as 1.5 million tons by some estimates. A portion of this treasure was turned over to Asante's skilled gold workers, whose creations celebrated the wealth and grandeur of the nation.

The Golden Stool, Asante's symbol of national unity, rests on its side, a practice designed to ward off harmful spirits. The small figures attached to the stool represent enemies slain in battle, and the bells are employed to summon the king's ancestors.

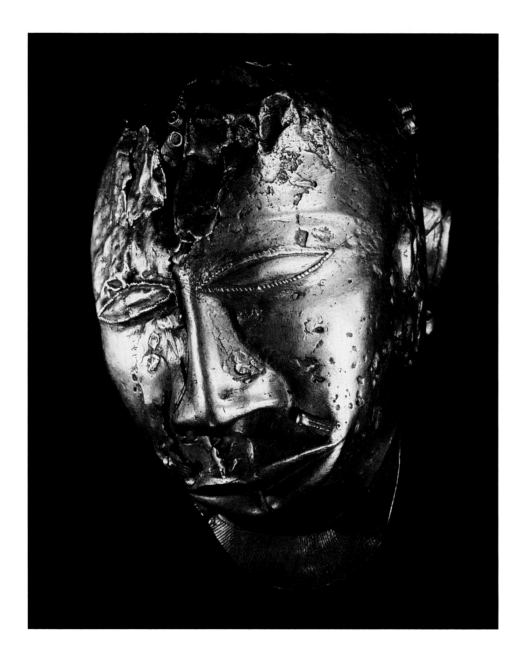

This golden head (measuring about seven inches long) belonged to the collection of the 19th-century asantehene Kofi Kakari and may have been used as an ornament on a royal sword.

27

*A kuduo, or brass
container, used for
storing gold dust
or other valuables.
The figure on top
of the container
represents a
crocodile, a denizen
of the rivers flowing
through Asante
territory.*

28

A guli *mask, representing the sun, created by a Baule goldsmith. The Baule, closely related to the Asante, live in the present-day Ivory Coast; according to tradition, the Baule kingdom was founded by an Asante princess during the 18th century.*

(Continued from page 24)

discharging their weapons, the musketeers would quickly turn and sprint toward the rear. It took at least 30 seconds to reload the guns, so the support troops would hold the line until the musketeers were ready to move forward and fire another volley.

As they pursued their conquests, the Asante were no more popular among their neighbors than the Denkyira had been a century earlier. A Muslim writer from Gonja, one of the northern states forced to pay tribute to Asante, recorded the following observation for the year 1750:

> In that year, Opoku, king of the Asante, died, may Allah curse him and place his soul in hell. It was he who injured the people of Gonja, oppressing them and robbing them of their property at will. He ruled violently, as a tyrant, delighting in his authority. People of all the horizons feared him greatly.

By the time of Opoku Ware's death, Kumase had become the center of a formidable empire. The city had taken its name from the *kuma* tree planted at its founding (Kumase literally means "under the kuma tree"). The tree was thought to contain the spirit of the asantehene, and the sight of it filled Kumase's citizens with a sense of power and well-being. When the aged tree was later toppled by a powerful windstorm, many Asante saw the event as an omen of impending doom.

By the 18th century, Kumase's population had grown to 25,000, and on special occasions, when people from the surrounding areas would come to attend great festivals, the total could swell to more than 100,000. The population was strictly divided according to social status: the three main divisions in Asante society were the nobility *(adeheyea)*, ordinary citizens *(amanmufo)*, and workers, or "people of the hearth" *(gyaasefo)*. Soldiers occupied elaborate camps outside the city, and the slaves who worked the fields and manned the gold mines lived in their own settlements, separated from the general citizenry.

The social position of an Asante was often revealed by his or her manner of dress. For centuries, the Akan had excelled at the art of weaving, and most of their garments were fashioned from high-quality cotton cloth. Not surprisingly, the finest cloths were reserved for the asantehene and the nobility, who sometimes added imported silks to their wardrobe. Most

A street in Kumase leading to the royal palace. The raised designs in the upper part of the houses were made by attaching vines to the outer wall and covering them with a thin layer of plaster.

30

women simply wrapped a length of cloth *(ntoma)* around their waist, creating a skirt that reached to the knees; those with small children might wear another cloth around their upper body, arranging the material to function as a child carrier. Men's cloths tended to be longer; they were not only wrapped around the body but also could be passed over the left shoulder so that they resembled the togas worn by the citizens of ancient Rome. Apart from the value of the cloth used in their garments, the distinction between classes was made clear by the amount and quality of the jewelry and other adornments worn by men and women alike.

Kumase contained 27 major thoroughfares, some of which were 600 yards long and 30 yards wide. Trees lined all the major streets, providing ample shade. The houses were usually one-story homes with open verandas that could be reached by a small flight of steps leading up from the street. The plastered and whitewashed walls were often covered with designs fashioned in bright red clay, and the roofs were constructed of bamboo poles covered with palm leaves. As the roofs extended well past the walls, they protected the elaborately decorated walls from the rain. A European visitor remarked that the arrangement of the houses "gives the streets a peculiar aspect of cheerfulness."

The royal palace was a massive complex of buildings constructed around a series of courtyards. It covered about five acres and contained many conveniences, including kitchens, bathhouses, and indoor lavatories. The center of the palace was the Pramaso, or Great Court, where the Council of Kumase met each day to make government decisions in concert with the asantehene. The windows of the various palace buildings were set in ornately carved panels, and some of the window frames were inlaid with gold.

Just outside the palace was the great market. In addition to its commercial function, the market was the social center of Kumase, akin to the

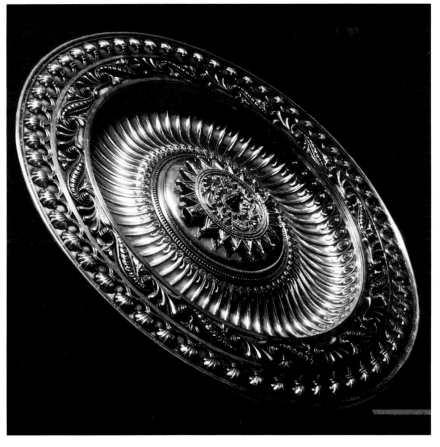

Gold disks such as this one were worn as pendants by the younger servants of the king. Those who carried such insignia were known as the king's "souls" (akra) and were generally being groomed for higher office.

main street of the smaller villages. Every night, royal musicians entered the market and played a fanfare to indicate that one day had ended and another had begun. The market was

31

32

also used for military parades, the display of captured enemies, and the reception of important visitors.

By all accounts, Kumase was remarkably well run, with vigorous measures taken to clean the streets and maintain public order. A host of rules were in effect throughout the capital, and violators could expect harsh punishment from the asantehene's officers. Some of the rules were clearly safety measures, such as the prohibition against building houses with grass roofs, which would have created a fire hazard. Other rules seemed arbitrary but were probably connected to religious practices or designed to maintain the distinction between social classes: citizens were forbidden to drop an egg in the street or to spill even a drop of palm oil; to smoke a European pipe; to whistle; to be in the street when the asantehene's wives passed by; or to mistake the name of a chief when addressing him.

In various places throughout the city, a number of circular platforms *(sumpene)* were placed for the use of the asantehene when he appeared among the people. On those occasions, the asantehene would sit beneath the shade of a huge umbrella, surrounded by his leading officials, and greet his subjects while drinking palm wine, which he shared with those who came up to greet him. During the Adae festival, held twice during each 42-day Asante month in honor of the nation's ancestors, the asantehene usually handed out gifts of gold dust to leading citizens.

Visitors to Kumase were above all struck by the lavish display of wealth in the royal court and in the society in general. Kumase was in every sense a city of gold, and the glittering display in its streets far exceeded anything to be seen in the cities of Europe. One European who attended a festival in Kumase provided the following descriptions of the asantehene and his entourage:

> The sun was reflected, with a glare scarcely more supportable than the heat, from the massy gold ornaments, which glistened in every direction . . . and massy gold necklaces, intricately wrought; suspended Moorish charms, dearly purchased and enclosed in small square cases of gold, silver, and curious embroidery. Gold and silver pipes, and canes dazzled the eye in every direction. Wolves and rams heads as large as life, cast in gold, were suspended from their gold

handled swords, which were held around them in great numbers.

Such displays of wealth were the outward sign of a prosperous and civilized society that enjoyed the spectacle of its own success. The continuation of that success, however, depended on the ability of the Asante to grapple with the demands of an empire. To this end, the administrative reforms begun by Opoku Ware at the beginning of the 18th century were further refined by Osei Kwadwo at the century's end.

Osei Kwadwo clearly believed that Asante could not maintain its position solely by force of arms. During his 13-year reign (1764–77), he shifted authority in many areas from military leaders to civilian officials. The Asante devoted great care to the training of these administrators. Many officials entered government departments as children and spent years performing menial jobs as they absorbed the routines and attitudes of public service. Though most of these youths were the sons of officials, Osei Kwadwo saw to it that opportunities were created for talented outsiders. Trainees who showed

This 19th-century engraving depicts an Asante diplomat attended by a small boy. One of the keys to Asante's success was the recruitment of children into the civil service, where they could learn the arts of statecraft by serving experienced officials.

33

ability were promoted, and the most capable eventually attained important posts. Under the guidance of these individuals, Asante entered the 19th century as the most sophisticated society in all of Africa.

Chapter 4 | THE QUILLS OF THE PORCUPINE

A 19th-century engraving depicts the annual Odwira festival in Kumase. Though it was the scene of much revelry, the festival also had a serious religious purpose —the spiritual purification of Asante.

The administration of Asante's wide domain depended on efficient communication, and the officials in Kumase took great pains to link the components of their empire. Affairs of state were conducted along the eight "great roads" that radiated from Kumase—four led to the south and the European outposts, four connected the capital to the trading centers of the north. A group of officials known as *nkwanmofo* had the job of keeping the routes open. This was a considerable task because of the enveloping forest and the torrential downpours of the rainy season; periodically, nkwanmofo would organize villagers to clear fallen trees and other debris from the roadway. In return for their cooperation, the villagers were allowed to sell food and other supplies to travelers.

The security of the roads was entrusted to the *nkwansrafo*, who functioned as highway police, collecting tolls and taxes from merchants, checking the identities of travelers, and keeping the roads free of bandits. An English visitor who traveled in Asante during the 1850s testified to the efficiency of these officers, noting that "the paths and thoroughfares of the country became so safe for the transmission of merchandise, and as free from interruptions of any description, as the best frequented roads of the most highly civilized countries of Europe."

Thousands of couriers (*afenasoafo*), identified by a particular type of sword issued only to those in public service,

36

This group of Asante officials includes a high-ranking ambassador (left), identified by his elaborate gold sword. The Asante placed great value on diplomacy; during the 19th century, they tried to create a union of West African states in the hope of curtailing European expansion.

traveled the great roads conducting government business. Because horses could not survive in the tsetse-infested forest belt, the afenasoafo traveled on foot. Owing to the ruggedness of the terrain and the various "unfavorable" days in the 42-day Asante month when travel was forbidden, it took about 20 days for a courier to make the round-trip from Kumase to the coast.

Government officials knew the amount of time it would take a courier to reach any given location within Asante, and they made plans and decisions on this basis. When a courier was dispatched on a mission, he was told to return to Kumase by a certain date. If the courier was long overdue, a second messenger might be sent out to determine the cause of the delay. In the most serious matters, where an ambassador had gone to settle a dispute with a tributary state, a long delay could mean that the ambassador had been taken prisoner or harmed. At that point, the asantehene might order his troops to invade the region in question.

Though periodic warfare was always an integral part of life in West Africa, 19th-century Asante—under such leaders as Osei Bonsu, Osei Yaw, and Kwaku Dua I—enjoyed generally

(Continued on page 41)

TIMELESS GLORY

Though the political power once wielded by the asantehene and his council has now passed to the central government of Ghana, the Asante have not abandoned their cultural and religious traditions. The elaborate insignia that dazzled European visitors during the great days of the Asante empire are still in use by Asante rulers and their attendants.

This royal attendant wears an eagle-feather headdress decorated with a set of golden ram's horns. The attendant's function is to carry the ceremonial sword on which Asante chiefs swear allegiance to the king.

A royal spokesman (okyeame) *holds the gold-plated spokesman's staff* (okyeame poma)*. In former days, the okyeame had a powerful influence on government decisions; today, his role is mainly ceremonial and includes advising rulers on traditions and rituals.*

A procession of sword bearers attending the chief of Kumawu. The design of these sword handles—twin globes separated by a cylindrical grip—dates back at least as far as the 16th century.

The chief of Kumawu sits beneath a state umbrella. Wearing a robe of kente cloth and adorned with resplendent gold jewelry, the kumawuhene embodies the grandeur of the Asante empire.

(Continued from page 36)

peaceful relations with neighboring kingdoms. The Asante did not try to extend their boundaries beyond the limits established during the 18th century, and powerful neighbors such as Dahomey and Wagadugu were not inclined to test the strength of Asante's army. Indeed, the Asante often referred to their nation as Kotoko, "the porcupine," proudly comparing themselves to the forest creature whose razor-sharp quills deterred even the fiercest animals from attacking it.

The Asante placed great value on diplomacy, and all leading officials were adept at public speaking and the art of negotiating. There is evidence that the Asante even tried to create an alliance of West African states, hoping to combat the growing power of Europeans on the Gold Coast. Ambassadors (bearing golden swords as symbols of their authority) were sent as far as the Muslim states of Massina and Segu on the upper Niger to discuss regional security measures. Unfortunately for the Asante, the other nations did not respond to these diplomatic efforts.

Perhaps the most important function of the officials traveling the great roads of Asante was the collection of taxes and death duties. All these payments were made in gold dust, the only form of currency accepted in Asante. (In many other West African states, such items as cowrie shells, strips of cloth, and iron bracelets known as manillas were used to pay for goods.) The basic monetary unit was the *peredwan*, equal to two and a quarter ounces of gold. Any large nuggets of gold found by miners or by people panning for gold in rivers and streams had to be turned over to government agents, who offered gold dust as compensation. The nuggets were then transported back to Kumase, where as many as 100 workers were employed in reducing the nuggets to gold dust. This dust was then deposited in the Adaka Kese, or Great Chest. Seven feet long, three feet high, and two feet wide, the Great Chest could hold up to 400,000 ounces of gold—a vast fortune by the standards of the time.

The tax collectors were known to all by the leather satchels they carried. In these satchels, they transported bags of gold dust as well as weights and scales for determining payments. The tax collectors were allowed to keep 15 percent of the gold they collected, so

A gold sword ornament depicting a porcupine, which served as a symbol of the Asante nation. Taking pride in their military might, the Asante often compared their warriors to the quills of the porcupine, stating, "Thousands may fall, but thousands more will grow."

they had an incentive to make sure that taxes were paid in full. They were always on the lookout for counterfeiters. Citizens trying to evade taxes were known to mix ground-up copper, silver, or coral with their gold dust; in order to detect these tricks, the collector might put a quantity of dust in a bowl and blow upon it, which caused the lighter materials to separate.

Because gold was so crucial to the life of Asante, counterfeiting was punishable by death. The historian Ivor Wilks has cited a dramatic example of the intense loathing Asante officials felt for those who indulged in trickery:

Reference is still made in Asante [as of 1979] to the unusual case of Akuroponhene Gyamfi Kwadwo, who purported during his lifetime to be a man of much wealth. He died in the later 1820s, but when his estate was appraised for death duties it was found to consist largely of counterfeit. The Asantehene Osei Yaw . . . ordered the corpse of Gyamfi Kwadwo to be exhumed; it was placed on trial, pronounced guilty, and beheaded.

The accurate weighing of gold dust was achieved through the use of carefully calibrated weights. The standard weights for the entire kingdom were kept in Kumase and guarded by the kingdom's chief financial officer, the *fotosanfohene*. All those even remotely involved in commerce, from government agents to the most humble tradesmen, possessed a personal set of weights. These objects represent one of the most distinctive aspects of Asante culture.

Though the Asante weight system had originated in North Africa and was

A collection of spoons used for weighing gold dust in Asante. Gold dust was the only form of currency used by the Asante, and great care was taken to ensure accuracy in tax payments and commercial dealings; counterfeiting was often punished by death.

43

introduced into Asante by Wangara traders during the 15th century, the Asante refined it into an exquisite art form. Weights were made of brass and cast in an astonishing variety of forms. Many were simple geometric figures. Others represented musical instruments, such as horns, drums, and flutes. Animals were also a popular subject, especially birds, fish, antelopes, leopards, and elephants. Numerous weights depicted people performing various everyday activities, such as cooking, farming, mining, carrying firewood, and hunting.

Asante craftsmen created these weights by using the lost-wax method of metal casting, a technique employed brilliantly by a number of other peoples in the West African forest belt, especially the Yoruba and the Edo. To make a gold weight, the artist would first fashion a model of the object, using wax that was gathered from the hives of wild bees. After carefully etching all the fine details into the wax, the artist would cover the figure with several layers of clay, creating a mold. When the mold was placed in the oven the clay would harden, and the wax would melt and run out, leaving a cavity in the center. Molten brass was then poured into the top of the mold, filling the space where the wax had been. When the brass cooled, the artist cracked open the mold and removed the finished sculpture.

In some cases, artists made the smallest weights by encasing a natural object, such as a leaf or a beetle, in layers of clay. When the mold was heated, the object would disintegrate, and the resulting sculpture would be a perfect brass replica of the original.

In addition to being beautiful and useful, the Asante weights also conveyed a message to those who used them. The language of the Asante was rich in proverbs, and many of the weights were designed to illustrate these sayings. One weight, for example, portrayed a man scraping bark off a tree. (Certain kinds of tree bark could be processed to make cloth.) The proverb evoked by this figure stated, "When a man goes alone to scrape bark from a tree, it falls to the ground." In other words, people must cooperate in order to be successful. A bird looking backward illustrated the proverb, "When it lies behind you, take it," meaning that the wisdom of the past could be valuable. The figure of an elephant suggested the saying, "One who

A selection of Asante gold weights, indicating the wide variety of designs employed by Asante artists. Many of the weights illustrated proverbs concerning personal conduct and social relations.

45

follows the track of the elephant never gets wet from the dew on the bushes"— by following an important man, a person will be shielded from harm.

These proverbs were known throughout Asante, and as Malcolm McLeod has indicated, they played a crucial role in the life of the nation:

> Knowledge of such sayings was essential for a person to advance in Asante society. They were thought to represent traditional wisdom and served to sway debates and clinch arguments. Senior men and women, and especially chiefs and officials, were expected to know dozens, even hundreds, of these sayings, and in the old days friendly competitions were held to see who knew the most, each person trying to cap the saying offered by the preceding person.

The intellectual richness and political refinement of Asante society were reflected most of all in the festivals and other public events that occurred with regularity in Kumase and other communities. Thomas Bowdich, who went to Kumase in 1817 to arrange a trade agreement for the British, was dazzled by the sights and sounds of these lavish displays:

What we had seen on our way [to Kumase] had made us expect something unusual. But we were still surprised by the extent and display of the scene which burst upon us here. An area of nearly a mile in circumference was crowded with magnificence and novelty. The king, his chiefs and captains, were splendidly dressed, and were surrounded by attendants of every kind. More than a hundred bands broke into music on our arrival. At least a hundred large umbrellas, each of which could shelter thirty persons, were sprung up and down by their bearers with a brilliant effect, being made in scarlet, yellow and the brightest cloths and silks, and crowned on top with crescents, pelicans, elephants, barrels, arms and swords of gold.

At the asantehene's country residence outside Kumase, a magnificent banquet was served on silver dishes, while musicians in blue-and-red uniforms played pieces they had learned from Dutch instructors. "We never saw a dinner more handsomely served, and never ate a better," Bowdich recorded.

At this time, the most impressive sight in all of Kumase may have been the Aban, or Palace of Culture, a large stone building erected by Osei Bonsu

46

in 1822. Thomas Freeman, a British missionary, visited the Aban in 1841 and reported the following:

> We entered a court yard, ascended a flight of stone steps, and passed through an ante-room into a small hall, in which were tastefully arranged on tables thirty-one gold-handled swords. In the same room were several of the King's calabashes, overlaid with gold, out of which he drinks palm-wine. Passing into another room, we found the King seated in company with Osai Kujoh, and attended by Apoko, and other linguists [councillors]. On tables in different parts of the room various articles manufactured in glass were arranged, such as candle-shades, beautifully cut glass tumblers, wine-glasses, etc.; and almost every piece was decorated with golden ornaments of various descriptions.

Freeman made his visit at a time when Asante and the British were at peace. However, the two nations had fought a bitter war 17 years earlier, and Britain's determination to control the Gold Coast was finally to bring about the ruin of the Aban and the rest of Kumase.

47

Chapter 5 | A CENTURY OF CONFLICT

Asante troops fire upon their British adversaries during a battle in 1874. Though the Asante were unmatched in courage and discipline, the British enjoyed a significant advantage in firepower.

Beginning in the 1440s, when Portuguese mariners first reached the West African coast, Europeans had been vigorously pursuing profit and influence in Africa. The Swedes, Danes, Germans, French, Dutch, and British had all followed the Portuguese example, establishing trading posts in the coastal areas along the Atlantic Ocean and the Gulf of Guinea. Between 1600 and 1850, slaves became the principal commodity along this coast, and European ships transported millions of able-bodied Africans to the Americas, where their labor and skills played a major role in the building of the New World.

Asante itself avoided the ravages of the transatlantic slave trade, which disrupted and degraded many African societies. Because of their wealth in gold, the Asante had actually been purchasers of slaves since the 15th century. When they felt that their slave population was becoming too large, they even sold off the excess to Europeans. Certainly no European entertained the idea of trying to seize slaves or gold from Asante. By the 19th century, the Asante could put as many as 200,000 men in the field, all armed with muskets and highly trained. As anthropologist Robert B. Edgerton has written:

> [Asante] troops marched with precision and maneuvered precisely, their muskets held at exactly the same slope, and they fired volleys on their officers' orders. . . . The Asante accomplishment in forging a

strictly disciplined army is the more remarkable because its common soldiers were slaves, many of whom had only recently been captured. . . . Yet when these men were on campaign they were somehow made to obey their officers, and they fought superbly. We can only marvel at the organizational genius that made this possible.

Edgerton points out that in addition to their prowess in battle, Asante troops also made an imposing and intimidating impression at formal military displays:

Each officer wore an immense cap topped by three foot-long plumes of eagle feathers, with gilded rams' horns thrusting out to the front. On their chests they wore red cloth vests covered with amulets of gold and silver, as well as various small brass bells, shells, and knives that jangled as they moved. Three or four animals' tails hung down from each arm, and long leopards' tails dangled down their backs. . . . A quiver of poisoned arrows hung from their right wrists, and each man brandished a small spear covered with red cloth and silk tassels in his left hand. They wore loose cotton trousers that were stuffed into soft, red leather boots reaching to mid-thigh, where they were attached by small chains to cartridge belts worn around the waist.

By the beginning of the 19th century, however, Great Britain was beginning to rival the Asante in military strength. Despite the loss of their American colonies in 1781, the British were emerging as Europe's greatest power and were vigorously exploiting the wealth of Asia, Africa, and the Middle East. The riches of the Gold Coast were among Africa's most alluring prizes.

At first, the British attempted to weaken Asante's power through political maneuvering. Bowdich's 1817 mission to Kumase resulted in the signing of a treaty that guaranteed the Asante access to the valuable coastal trade routes. Though the Asante took this promise at face value, the British had only offered the treaty in order to pacify the Asante while they plotted against them. They immediately formed an alliance with the Fante, who had long been enemies of the Asante, and encouraged the Fante to block Asante's access to the coast. When the Asante asserted their rights under the 1817 treaty, the British brushed aside these appeals and made it clear that they would defend the Fante against any Asante attack.

Asante's attempts to subdue the Fante involved a number of skirmishes with British troops, but moderate forces in Asante, led by Asantehene Osei Bonsu, managed to stave off a major conflict for several years. The peaceful interlude came to an end in 1822, when Sir Charles MacCarthy assumed command of British forces on the Gold Coast. MacCarthy believed that he could crush the Asante without much difficulty, and in January 1824 he led a small force against the Asante armies near the Pra River. The Asante easily routed their enemies, who included black slaves from the British islands in the Caribbean and detachments of Fante. MacCarthy was wounded in the battle, and when he realized that he was about to be captured, he killed himself. The victorious Asante beheaded the British commander and kept his skull on display in Kumase for many years.

When Osei Bonsu died, the prowar faction in Kumase gained strength. The new asantehene, Osei Yaw, was more inclined to fight than negotiate, and he soon led Asante's troops against the Fante and other British allies in the south. In 1826, British and Asante forces met again at

This 19th-century engraving depicts an Asante officer in elaborate ceremonial dress, which includes eagle feathers, leopard tails, and red leather boots. The small knives worn at the waist were used to decapitate slain enemies.

51

Katamanso. This time the British, having amassed a larger force equipped with devastating rocket launchers, carried the day. The defeat weakened Asante's authority in the south, but the stability and power of the kingdom itself was unaffected.

After Katamanso, advocates of

A British artist, looking out on Kumase from the roof of the Aban on February 5, 1874, sketched this scene of chaos and destruction as British troops set fire to the city.

peace once again gained the upper hand, both in Kumase and in London. In 1831, Britain and Asante signed a new treaty, ushering in a reign of peace that lasted for more than 40 years.

Unfortunately, no treaty could curb Britain's desire for expansion. The death knell for peace on the Gold Coast came in 1872, when the British took control of Elmina, the long-standing Dutch outpost on the Gulf of Guinea, and became the preeminent European power on the Gold Coast. A year later, the British government appointed Sir Garnet Wolseley to command their

forces on the Gold Coast. Wolseley lost little time in preparing a major expedition against Kumase. Kofi Kakari and his advisers decided to fight a defensive action at Amoafo, about 25 miles south of the capital. The battle was joined on January 30, 1874.

Skillfully concealing themselves in the forest, the Asante stopped the attackers in their tracks with withering volleys of rifle fire. Wolseley himself, who later called the Asante campaign "the most horrible war I ever fought," freely admitted that the Asante would have wiped out his infantry if not for the huge advantage in firepower enjoyed by the British. Unable to update their weaponry because of Britain's stranglehold on the coastal ports, the Asante were still using their antiquated muskets. The British—in addition to their rockets—were now equipped with highly efficient rapid-fire rifles. Gradually, the Asante were forced to fall back, and on February 3, British forces entered a nearly deserted Kumase. After the British looted the royal palace and torched the city, Kofi Kakari sent a message to Wolseley asking for peace and agreeing to recognize British authority over the Gold Coast.

In the aftermath of the war, Kofi

Kakari was forced to abdicate in favor of Mensa Bonsu, but the change was not enough to hold Asante together. With the active encouragement of the British, most of Asante's tributary states declared their independence from Kumase, and in 1883, a two-year civil war broke out, devastating what remained of the once-great Asante union. Only in the 1890s did the Asante begin to reunite and rebuild their economy under the rule of Prempe I.

Naturally, the British viewed Asante's resurgence with alarm. They were especially fearful of a possible Asante alliance with the French, who were pursuing their own interests in West Africa. In 1896, a British force boldly marched into Kumase, arrested Prempe I, and shipped him off to exile in the Seychelles Islands, a British possession off the coast of East Africa. Even this setback failed to cripple the Asante recovery, and four years later, the British demanded the surrender of the Golden Stool itself. Such an act was unthinkable for the Asante, and they mounted a powerful last-ditch attempt to drive the British from the Gold Coast. This time, the British had an even greater advantage in weaponry,

having added both machine guns and artillery to their arsenal. The Asante managed to hide the Golden Stool, but they could not preserve their independence against the massive firepower of the enemy. As the 20th century began, Asante became part of the British Empire.

The British usually governed their colonies through local leaders, and by 1924, they were confident enough to restore Prempe I to the Golden Stool, though they made it clear that his power did not extend beyond Kumase. Much had changed in Asante during the asantehene's absence, as is evident from Robert Edgerton's account of his return:

> British officials met him with appropriate ceremony when he left the ship, and a special train took him to Kumase, where he was met by a huge throng of Asante wearing white clothes, their faces painted with white stripes as a sign of joy. When he stepped off the train, there were loud cheers, and many people wept with joy. He was dressed in a European suit, and despite the heat, he wore a wool overcoat. As they greeted him, he smiled and lifted his black-felt homburg to them. He then stepped into a waiting automobile, which

53

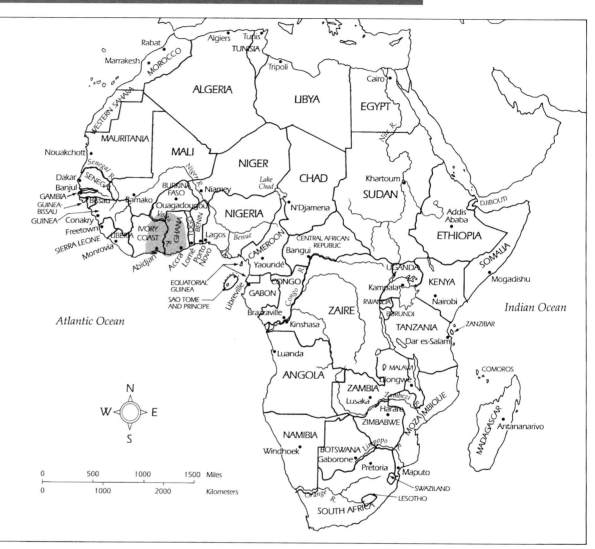

A map of present-day Africa, with the shaded area indicating the former territory of Asante. The previous borders of the Asante empire correspond almost exactly to those of the modern nation of Ghana.

took him to a house that had been prepared for him.

Like their ruler, the Asante adapted quickly to the forces of 20th-century life. Considering their age-old organizational genius and the unifying power of the Golden Stool, it is not surprising that the Asante played the leading role in the drive for African self-rule that followed the end of World War II in 1945. In 1957, the nation of Ghana was born, taking its name from the first of West Africa's great kingdoms. The borders of the new nation were almost identical with the former territory of Asante. Akan-speaking peoples comprised nearly half of Ghana's population, creating a powerful force for political and cultural unity.

Under the leadership of its first president, Kwame Nkrumah, Ghana became a powerful inspiration to all nations struggling against colonial domination. The Akan goldfields remained highly productive, and with the export of such commodities as cocoa and rubber, Ghana emerged as one of Africa's most prosperous nations. Though gold weights were no longer a necessity with the adoption of paper currency, Asante goldsmiths and weavers continued to excel at their craft, and Ghanaian kente cloth gradually became a popular fashion item throughout the world.

Though the capital of Ghana is the coastal city of Accra, Kumase is now a thriving city of 800,000 and is the home of the University of Science and Technology, one of Ghana's three major

55

universities. The great kuma tree may be long gone, but the Adae festival is still celebrated twice a month, and on these occasions the asantehene—still the leader of his people, even though final political authority rests with the central government—greets his subjects and other visitors in the Prempe II Jubilee Museum, which celebrates the history of a people whose greatest days may still be ahead of them.

A view of the Ashanti Gold Fields Corporation mining complex at Obuasi, Ghana, in 1962.

CHRONOLOGY

c. 1000 B.C.	Akan-speaking peoples settle in the valley of the Volta River
14th century	Akan establish trade relations with savanna states
15th century	Akan begin to exploit their goldfields with imported slave labor; clear large areas of forest for farming; start to live in large settlements headed by chiefs
16th century	Akan living in the gold-rich Adanse hills expand northward, establishing new states and calling themselves the Asante
1650	Neighboring state of Denkyira defeats the Asante in battle; Asante forced to pay tribute to the king of Denkyira
1690	Osei Tutu becomes the ruler of the Asante and unifies his people with the symbol of the Golden Stool
1701	Asante defeat Denkyira in battle and become the major power among the Akan
1720–50	Reign of Opoku Ware, who creates national treasury and death duties; Asante expand their territory into an empire
1764–77	Reign of Osei Kwadwo, who develops the government of Asante to its highest level of sophistication and efficiency

1817	Asante sign treaty with British government, but Britain begins campaign to destroy Asante influence on the Gold Coast
1824	Asante defeat British troops commanded by Sir Charles MacCarthy
1826	British defeat Asante at Battle of Katamanso and take control of trade routes in the south
1831	Britain and Asante sign new treaty, ushering in 43-year period of peace
1874	British forces under Sir Garnet Wolseley sack Kumase and force Asante to recognize British power on the Gold Coast
1896	British forces arrest Asante ruler Prempe I and send him into exile
1900	Asante make final, unsuccessful attempt to repel British forces; Asante becomes part of the British Empire
1957	Ghana becomes first African nation to achieve independence from colonial rule; Asante are the dominant ethnic group of the new nation

FURTHER READING

Arhin, Kwame. "The Structure of Greater Ashanti." *Journal of African History* 8 (1967), 65–85.

Bosman, William. *A New and Accurate Description of the Coast of Guinea.* Reprint of the 1705 edition. London: Cass, 1967.

Bowdich, T. E. *Mission from Cape Coast Castle to Ashantee.* Reprint of the 1819 edition. London: Cass, 1966.

Connah, Graham. *African Civilizations.* Cambridge: Cambridge University Press, 1987.

Davidson, Basil. *Africa in History.* Rev. ed. New York: Collier, 1991.

————. *The African Genius.* Boston: Little, Brown, 1969.

Davidson, Basil, with F. K. Buah and the advice of J. F. A. Ajayi. *A History of West Africa, 1000–1800.* New rev. ed. London: Longmans, 1977.

Edgerton, Robert B. *The Fall of the Asante Empire.* New York: Free Press, 1995.

Freeman, T. B. *Journal of Two Visits to the Kingdom of Ashanti.* Reprint of the 1843 edition. London: Cass, 1968.

Garrard, T. F. *Akan Weights and the Gold Trade.* London: Longman, 1980.

Hull, Richard W. *African Cities and Towns Before the European Conquest.* New York: Norton, 1976.

McEvedy, Colin. *The Penguin Atlas of African History.* New York: Penguin, 1980.

McLeod, Malcolm. *The Asante.* London: British Museum Publications, 1981.

Oliver, Roland, and Brian M. Fagan. *Africa in the Iron Age.* Cambridge: Cambridge University Press, 1975.

Park, Mungo. *Travels in the Interior Districts of Africa.* Reprint of the 1799 edition. New York: Arno Press/New York Times, 1971.

Rattray, R. S. *Ashanti.* Oxford: Clarendon Press, 1923.

———. *Ashanti Law and Constitution.* Oxford: Clarendon Press, 1929.

———. *Ashanti Proverbs.* Oxford: Clarendon Press, 1916.

———. *Religion and Art in Ashanti.* Oxford: Clarendon Press, 1927.

Smith, Robert. *Warfare and Diplomacy in Pre-Colonial West Africa.* 2nd ed. Madison: University of Wisconsin Press, 1989.

UNESCO General History of Africa. 8 vols. Berkeley: University of California Press, 1980–93.

Webster, J. B., and A. A. Boahen, with M. Tidy. *The Revolutionary Years: West Africa Since 1800.* New ed. London: Longman, 1980.

Wilks, Ivor. *Asante in the 19th Century.* New ed. Cambridge: Cambridge University Press, 1989.

———. *Forests of Gold: Essays on the Akan and the Kingdom of Asante.* Athens: University of Ohio Press, 1993.

GLOSSARY

Adae   festival held twice during each 42-day Asante month; its purpose is to honor the Asante's ancestors

Akan   language spoken by the Asante of Ghana and other peoples of the West African forest belt

akonnua   a carved wooden stool that symbolizes the authority of the asantehene

asantehene   literally, "chief of the Asante"; title used by the ruler of Asante since the late 17th century

clan   a social group united by descent from a common ancestor; also known as a descent line

colony   territory controlled by a foreign nation, which exploits the region's resources and people for profit

Gold Coast   name used by European traders to designate the coastal region of Akan territory; later the name of the British colony in the region, which is now the independent nation of Ghana

Golden Stool   the ultimate symbol of nationhood and royal authority among the Asante

hunter-gatherers   people who live in small groups, harvesting wild plants and hunting game animals; common way of life before the development of iron tools

kola	an African tree yielding nuts that contain a stimulant similar to caffeine
lost-wax	method of metal casting used to make the brass gold-weights common throughout Asante
musketeer	a soldier armed with a musket, an early firearm
Odwira	annual festival held in Kumase; included ceremonies designed to enhance the spiritual powers of the king
proverb	a short saying that contains wisdom or humor; common in the Akan language
savanna	the broad grassland extending across sub-Saharan Africa from the Atlantic Ocean to the Nile Valley
tribute	a payment from one person or nation to another as a sign of submission or a guarantee of protection
Wangara	Muslim traders from the empire of Mali who supplied the Asante with slaves and material goods in exchange for gold

INDEX

PHILIP KOSLOW earned his B.A. and M.A. degrees from New York University and went on to teach and conduct research at Oxford University, where his interest in medieval European and African history was awakened. The editor of numerous volumes for young adults, he is also the author of *El Cid* in the Chelsea House HISPANICS OF ACHIEVEMENT series and *Centuries of Greatness: The West African Kingdoms, 750–1900* in the Chelsea House series MILESTONES IN BLACK AMERICAN HISTORY.

PICTURE CREDITS